# BUILD YOUR OWN TREE

## BREAKING GENERATIONAL CURSES

## DANALIS ANDERSON

Build Your Own Tree
Copyright © 2019 by Danalis Anderson



ISBN: 9781513642758

Printed in USA by Spark 2 Inspire Publishing

# Dedication

I dedicate this book to my Lord and savior who is the head of my life. Without the Lord I am nothing. I want to also dedicate my book to my 91 year old Grandmother Eartha Johnson. She is a mighty woman of God. She taught me how to pray and be strong. My grandmother is the only 91 year old that I know that is still an usher. I love you MaMa for playing a huge part in my life. I also want to dedicate this book to my Husband Anthony Anderson of 21 years. He prays for me and pushes me to keep going. He has supported me in everything I have done. I love you Mr. Anderson. Our children Dr. Shantae Motley that wouldn't let me give up. Always making sure my spelling was right lol. Our son Kiante Anderson for praying for me, and our youngest daughter Aislynn that motivated me. They are my biggest cheerleaders. My big brother Lennie Motley for praying for me. My big little brother Anthony Mendez, whose main words to me was "You got this Dee" My other little brother's Ty'rese and Vernal Downing that's always excited for me. Last but not least my mother Rosa Downing. This woman right here has been my prayer partner, best friend, protector, motivator, I can go on and on about my mother. She has been such an awesome woman in my life. I'm not saying we are perfect, but by the grace of God he kept us.

# Table of Contents

# **FOREWARD**

It is my honor to be able to write the foreward for this book. It's not been long that I have known Pastor Danalis Anderson, but I know that she an awesome woman of God with a love for God and His people. It was at a prayer breakfast that I met Pastor Anderson and heard her say "Build Your Own Tree". It immediately resonated with me and I didn't really understand why.

After speaking with her and reading this book I fully recognize why it had such a powerful impact when I first heard it. I have spent the last 30 plus years trying to do exactly that,  I have been Building My Own Tree.  I continue to by intentionally working to break generational curses, while embracing generational blessings so that I could walk in the purpose and promises that God has for me.

God knows us and has a specific plan and purpose for each one of us. Unfortunately for many people life's circumstances and situations prevent them from experiencing everything that God has for them.  Jeremiah 29:11 For I know the plans I have for you" says the Lord. They are plans for good and not disaster, to give you a future and a hope. (NLT). When pain, hurt and tragedies come we lose sight of who God is and who we are.  The situations and circumstances paralyze us, and stop us from moving in the plan of God for our lives.  If you surrender all to God He will get you through. Not only will He get you through you will be better when you do. God loves us and cares for us. The tragedies of life will never change that. We need to keep our minds and our hearts fixed on Jesus so that we can become all that He wants us to be.  In fact I would say that the challenges that we face, help to shape us into what God wants us to be.  Over the last 10 years I have faced so many challenges, but I have continued to build despite the challenges. The challenges strengthen us and help us to become mature Christians, learning to surrender and trust Him. The challenges prepare us and equip us for the assignments that God has for us.

Pastor Anderson gives us a glimpse of her pain, battles and flaws and how she had to navigate through life to build her own tree. You to have the ability to do the same. You have to power through Christ Jesus to break generational curses and be free of any tragedy, pain or hurt that you have experienced in life.  Get ready to start building as Pastor Anderson takes you through the blue print of her life and how she Building Her Own Tree.

# PART 1

## INTRODUCTION

**I** decided to write this book Build Your Own Tree, when I realized that generational curses are taking over our lives. It is causing us to stop living, dreaming, trusting and loving people, and most importantly ourselves. I was talking to someone I knew and had not seen in a while. I began to celebrate her life accomplishments. The more we talked, her pain became more evident. She said "I want to be married, but in my family tree the women are only known for having babies. None of us are married." Before I knew it, the Holy Spirit led me to say BUILD YOUR OWN TREE. If you do not like the tree you are in, then build your own. Now I wasn't telling her to forget her old tree, because you never want to forget where you came from. Our families fought and prayed hard for us to get to where we are, but not all the times things came out the way they wanted it to, but they did their best to get us where we are now. Being raised in one of the hardest projects in Brooklyn NY made it hard to dream. We were taught to survive. There is no time to dream when you have to fight just to stay alive. Being brought up in a single home raised by my awesome amazing mom was hard. She worked full time and put herself through college. All while raising 2 children at the time. Then came 3. She did the best she could on what she had. She loved us so much and worked so hard to get us out the projects. Don't get me wrong. I don't look down at the projects because it helped me to be where I'm at today. That was the beginning of my tree. I knew it was more but I didn't know how to dream only to survive. Just know we can't plant what we been through. We can build where we are going. Just like the three little pigs. One chose to use straw to build their house. One chose to use sticks to build their house. Then one chose to use bricks to build their house. I tried the straw, and sticks.  It came down. Now I'm choosing bricks to build. Bricks are stronger so they stay together, and I can keep adding new bricks to build my legacy. Moving from survival mode to dreams coming true.  This first part of my story is giving you a little glimpse on how I survived, before I learned how to dream. I pray this will help you.

# Chapter One

## DEPRESSION

### Scripture: 2 Samuel 22:29 NKJV

For you are my lamp, O Lord: the Lord shall enlighten my darkness.

Depression: Depression is a mood disorder that causes persistent feelings of sadness and loss of interest. It affects how you feel, think, and behave and can lead to emotional and physical problems.

I remember the day when I realized I was depressed. My family and I were having family time in the living room. We were all laughing about something, but the whole time I was laughing I just wanted to cry. I did not know what was going on. I could not be depressed. I had it all together.  I had a husband, children, and a house. I thought I had it made. I came to realize that I was really good at covering up my emotions. I could not let anyone know that when I dropped my kids off to school I would close the shades, get in the bed and stay there until I picked them back up from school. I did that for a whole year. Oh, I forgot to tell you that during this time I was a believer of Christ, singing on the praise team, and in the choir. I used to be upset when nobody picked me up in the spirit. How could they though, I was good at covering it up. Nothing ever gets healed when you cover it up.  Not even my own family knew. I remember driving, and could not remember how I got home because my depression took over my thoughts. When I realized it I was in front of my house. I would just sit in the car trying to figure out how I got home. The days would go by and I didn't know what day it was. I would wake up 4am fix my husband's breakfast and lunch, kiss him, and with a smile watch him leave. I would then sit on the bed saying to myself why can't it stay night time. I have to pretend another day that I am ok when I am not. I just want to remind you again that I was a believer of Christ, singing on praise and worship team, and in the choir. As I went on my days turned into weeks then months. It started to get worse and soon I would just break down and cry in front of my husband. He would ask me what was wrong and I couldn't give him an answer. He would just hold me until I stopped crying. After doing that for some time, I finally said enough is enough. I have a family to be there for. I remember sitting in my living room and talking to God asking him for help because I refused to take medication. I refused to be locked up in a crazy house. I knew it was a spiritual fight when I went to seek help, and the Psychologist said he couldn't help me. He told me that I need to get spiritual help. I was like wow! Did he just say that to me? He didn't even charge me. So I had to make up in my mind that I would have to make a change in my life. I had to REFUSE to allow the enemy to take over my life. When I REFUSED is when the Lord stepped in. Now he was there all the time, but I had to want to get out of depression.  I fell prostate and began to pray. I cried out to the Lord so hard that I fell asleep. When I woke up it felt like a brand new day. Unfortunately the depression got so bad I wanted to take my own life.

Don't forget I said I was a believer of Christ sung on the praise team and in the choir, but, I wanted to take my own life. I had it all planned out. I was going take my kids to school and drive off of the bridge. Two words BUT GOD!!!! The plan was to take them to school come home write my goodbye letter and proceed with the plan. Well I'm here to say my plans wasn't God's plans. The bible says in Jeremiah 29:11 in the NIV "For I know the plans I have for you declares the Lord, plans to prosper and not to harm you, plans to give you hope and a future." Knowing this is his plan, my plan wasn't going to work out. The Lord allowed the phone to ring and it was my mother. We began to talk on the phone for an hour. As we were talking I began asking myself does she know what I'm thinking about doing. After I hung with her I started writing my letter. While I was writing the letter I was crying and next thing I knew I fell asleep. When I woke it up it was time to pick up my kids. I believe God put me in a deep sleep. I started to think what they would do without me.  I also figured once I leave this world they would live well with the insurance money. Later I found out that you can't get the insurance money if you take your own life. That devil is something else. The devil thought he had me. When I picked up my children from school and saw their faces light up when they saw me, I knew for sure I had to live for me as well as for my family. So when ever depression tries to creep up on me, I have to say I REFUSE to die. I had to share this with YOU, yes YOU. You have to REFUSE to live in depression. You have to take it day by day, hour by hour, minute by minute, and second by second. You have to take control over your life. You have to say I am not that story anymore. I am going to remove this from my tree. Please understand that the reason why I can share this with you is because I'm not that person anymore. I am now the person that REFUSED to die.

# I DECREE AND DELCARE
## (THAT DEPRESSION IS NOT APART OF MY TREE)

**Notes**

_______________________________________
_______________________________________
_______________________________________
_______________________________________
_______________________________________
_______________________________________
_______________________________________
_______________________________________
_______________________________________
_______________________________________
_______________________________________
_______________________________________
_______________________________________
_______________________________________
_______________________________________
_______________________________________
_______________________________________
_______________________________________
_______________________________________
_______________________________________
_______________________________________
_______________________________________
_______________________________________

# Chapter Two

## IDENTITY

## Scripture : Jeremiah 1:5 KJV

Before I formed thee in the belly I knew thee; and before thou camest forth out of the womb I sanctified thee, and I ordained thee a prophet unto the nations.

The definition of identity is who you are, the way you  think about yourself , the way you are viewed by the world and the characteristics that define you.

Now this one believe it or not is one of the hardest to write about, because it was just a couple of years ago that I found out who I was. I had been going about my life thinking I knew who I was and that I was on the right path. When I was born I was called baby, child, teenager and then teenage mom. Then I became a young adult to mom, and wife. I got trapped in the duties of life. I got lost in who I was to become. Those titles just gave me a name, but I was a broken, incomplete person. I was living by my circumstances, and who man said I was. I got lost in the maze. There was a way out, but I believed what man said I was. Man said I was dumb and that I would never be anything. So I started believing it and acting like it. Man said I was ugly and fat and that no one would ever love me and want me. So I started believing it. I would start things and get excited about it, and as soon as the devil would step in and say you can't, I would stop. When someone came into my life and said I was beautiful I would believe it, and fall into the trap. You know the trap, looking for love in all the wrong places. I tried to be someone that I wasn't to fit in. I then became an angry person. I felt like I had to fight my way through life to carry a name for myself, because of what others said about me. It really was hard when I became a teenage mom. My thought was now what are they going to say about me. One thing I can say was my mother always told me to keep my head up. I felt I embarrassed the family being 18 years old and pregnant. I know my mother wanted more for me. I know she wanted me to live and enjoy life before starting a family. Unfortunately, here I was pregnant in a home where there was only one parent taking care of 3, now 4. How could I put my family through this? Life was already hard, and I made it worse through my own choices. I shamed my family and added more pain to my brokenness.  This was the beginning of BUILDING MY OWN TREE. I had to grow up faster than I was supposed to. I had to now be an adult because I had to take care of my responsibilities. I couldn't deal with being broken, and incomplete. I had to prepare to be a mom. A teenage single mom. Are you seeing what's going on? It's called generational curses. My mom is a strong working person. She loves her family, but she's doing everything by herself. I don't believe she wanted to do it by herself, but at that time she had no other choice. Here I come adding more stress to her, and the family, but can I just say ONLY GOD! When my daughter was born. She changed our lives. She brought our family closer together. I can actually say she was the missing piece of the puzzle. I know my decision to become pregnant at a young age wasn't the right decision. I had no other choice then to grow up quickly and take care of my responsibilities. My mother didn't make it easy for me, and I thank her for that. She made me work, and buy clothes for myself every paycheck. When my daughter was born she made sure I got up to take care of her. I will never forget what she taught me. As time went by I had a husband and children to make happy. I had no time to fix my brokenness and my feelings of being incomplete, because it was no longer about me. It was about my family. I had to cover up what I was dealing with within me, and try to be the best mother, and wife I could be. So the years went on, and I watched my children grow up. I began to feel the brokenness and feelings of being incomplete surfacing again. Meanwhile I still believed the lies that people were, and had said to me.  In reality I was smart enough to work hard and take care of my daughter. I found someone that loved me and I loved him and made a family with him. The pieces of my brokenness started to come together. I got closer to the Lord. No longer was it religion, it was a relationship with the Lord. I started to feel whole and complete, and it was an amazing feeling. It was great beginning to understand that I wasn't who man said I was.  I started believing who God said I am. St. Matthew 16:13-17 NIV says when Jesus came to the region of Caesarea Philippi, he asked his disciples, "WHO DO PEOPLE SAY THE SON OF MAN IS? They replied, some say John the Baptist other say Elijah; and still others, Jeremiah or one of the prophets. Simon Peter answered, you are the Messiah, the son of the living God. Jesus already knew who he was and what his purpose was. Now I had to find out my purpose. I am so glad that I came to realize that tiles are not who you are. Who we are is fearfully and wonderfully made by God.  I am fearfully and wonderfully made.  My purpose is to show love and kindness to the world. My purpose is to be an ambassador of Christ, and to help others learn how to know themselves and find their purpose. As we stay in the will of God he will show us our purpose. I know what the world's definition says about identity, but we can't focus on how the world views us. We have to focus on how God views us. The bible says in Philippians 4:13 KJV, I can do all things through Christ that strengthens me. Knowing where our help comes from makes it easy to move forward.  This is when everything will begin to fall in place. I've removed broken and incomplete, and added whole and striving to be complete. My new tree is starting to bloom.

I DECREE AND DECLARE

(I KNOW WHO I AM)

## Notes

_______________________________________________

_______________________________________________

_______________________________________________

_______________________________________________

_______________________________________________

_______________________________________________

_______________________________________________

_______________________________________________

_______________________________________________

_______________________________________________

_______________________________________________

_______________________________________________

# Chapter Three

## FORGIVENESS

## Scripture: Ephesians 4:32 NIV

And be kind and compassionate to one another, forgiving each other, just as Christ God forgave you.

Forgiveness is for our own growth and happiness. When we hold on to hurt, pain, resentment, and anger it harms us far more than it harms the person that hurt you.

God, please help me while I write this because you are a forgiving God and you are teaching us how to have forgiveness in our hearts AMEN.

I had to start off with a prayer because forgiveness was one of the hardest things for me to do.  I felt like if I didn't forgive the one that took my innocence it would make me feel better. What I mean about my innocence is the person that raped me. He took something that didn't belong to him. It caused anger and hatred. Let me be honest I wanted revenge. So I felt like if I kept hatred in my heart I would hurt him. I realized that is not true. It didn't give me power or make me feel good, it actually held me hostage. Hostage in my mind, body, and soul. I felt like I was in prison locked up like he should have been. It caused me not to trust anyone for a long time. I always had my guard up towards people.  Really my guard was with men. I felt like all the men were alike. I felt like all men would take advantage of me, and eventually rape me. Having this in my heart was actually letting him rape me over and over mentally.  I had to finally realize that I was in a mental prison when I recognized that I would shut down around that time every year. I would get very emotional during this time and I realized that I also began holding my children hostage as well. I didn't really trust anyone to look after them or them staying at anyone's houses. It did not matter if they were family and friends. I felt like I could only protect them if I kept them close to me, but that wasn't right for them or me. Listen I'm not going to lie, I'm still protective over my children. I just don't hold them hostage now. I had to forgive that person. Forgiving him brought so much peace to my life.

I now know that as 2 Chronicles 20:15 NIV says, the battle is not yours, but God's. You might be saying you cannot relate because nothing like that has happened to you. I thank God it hasn't, but you might have a problem with forgiving a family member, friend, etc... I have been there, done that. Yes, it was hard just the thought of their name or face use to anger me. I couldn't believe that someone could purposely want to hurt me. When people use to say "that's not them, it's a spirit," I didn't want to hear it. I would plan to get revenge on them, but I had to realize that hurt people, hurt people, and a hurter is not who I am or was. When I began to pray for them as well as myself, God began to lift me up. God changed my way of thinking and feelings toward people that have hurt me. Now I can look at them and feel peace. Sometimes he allows me to forget what they did to me, and when I do remember it is a few days later. I remember I'm out of their presence. What I mean about that is God would allow me to be tested by allowing me to run into them. I would say hello, God bless you and move on. When I realized it I was at home saying God did you just show me that I am free?  I give God praise every time that happens. For me to allow my new tree to bloom I had to handle the things on my old tree. If you don't want to be a prisoner anymore you have to learn how to forgive and move on so you can have peace within yourself. You have to ask God for help to get rid of the things that are not pleasing to him daily. Trust me it's a process, but you have to trust the process by trusting God.


I DECREE AND DECLARE

(THAT FORGIVENESS IS IN MY HEART)


**Notes**

___________________________________________
___________________________________________
___________________________________________
___________________________________________
___________________________________________
___________________________________________
___________________________________________
___________________________________________
___________________________________________
___________________________________________
___________________________________________

# Chapter Four

## FEAR

## Scripture: 2 Timothy 1:7 KJV

For God hath not given us the spirit of fear but: of power and love, and of a sound mind.

Fear is an unpleasant emotion caused by the belief that someone or something is dangerous, likely to cause pain, or a threat. Fear had caused me not to trust anyone. I always thought someone was trying or planning to hurt me. What fear did was cause me to build a wall of protection. Living in one of the worse projects in Brooklyn, NY caused me to live in fear due to the killing, rapes, and muggings that occurred there. I used to live on the 12th floor and the elevators were always broken. When I would leave to go to school there were two different sets of stairs. I would run down one flight then run on the other side and run down that flight until I got to the bottom just in case someone was following me. This feeling of fear caused me to always stay in the house. My mother was in constant fear because she didn't want anything to happen to us.

I remember the first time I got mugged. I wore my chain that said #1 daughter. I was so happy to wear it and someone came up to me and snatched it off my neck. What a life to live right? I also remember when a group of us were walking home and a group of guys from other projects came up to us and sliced my friend in his face. I watched his face open up in front of me and it took such a long time to get that off my mind. It caused me to keep living in fear.

Growing up I lost one of my best friends. She got stabbed at a party and died. I went to her funeral and people starting shooting. I remember running for my life. I ended up at home with one shoe because I lost one while running. I didn't know it took such a toll on me until I realized I was watching my back all the time. That is not how God wants us to live. He wants us to know that he is shielding us. Ephesians 6:10-11 KJV says "finally my brethren, be strong in the Lord, and in the power of his might. Put on the whole armor of God ye may be able to stand against the wiles of the devil." The devil will have us living in fear. We have to learn to put our trust in God. I decided not to live in fear and to trust God. I began to quote this scripture Psalm 23: 4 KJV "yea, though I walk through the valley of the shadow of death, I will fear no evil: for thou art with me; thou rod and thy staff they comfort me." I thank God for comfort and protection.

I DECREE AND DECLARE

(I WILL NOT LIVE IN FEAR)

**NOTES**

______________________________________________

______________________________________________

______________________________________________

______________________________________________

______________________________________________

______________________________________________

# Chapter Five

## DOUBT

## Scripture: St. John 20:27 NIV

Then he said to Thomas, "put your finger here; see my hands. Reach out your hand and put it into my side. Stop doubting and believe.


Doubt is a feeling of not knowing what to believe, what to do or a condition of being uncertain. It seems as if all my life I would second guess what I could do. Why? It is because I always value what others thought about what I was doing and I never thought what I was doing was good enough. I remember when I wanted to start my business. I found myself asking other people what they thought. Then, when they shared their opinion and I did not like what they said, I got upset. I do not know why I got upset, because I chose to ask them about what I wanted to do in my life. I doubted what I could do, and then would get mad when someone did not tell me what I wanted to hear. Then, because I was upset, I would want to prove them wrong. That was not the right way to handle it for them or for myself. I had to believe and trust what I wanted to do was going to happen, and that I would be successful.

I remember also when I doubted that I would ever get married. People would say I would never amount to anything and nobody would ever want to marry me. I started to believe it and started dating people that I knew was cheating on me. One word, SETTLE. That is what I was doing. Settling, because of what others said about me. That's not what God wants for us. Jeremiah 29:11 NIV says "For I know the plans I have for you," declares the Lord. "Plans to prosper you and not to harm you, plans to give you hope and a future." This is what God wants. I had to stop doubting and trust him when he told me what he wanted me to do. I now do what he says without asking anyone else's opinion. When I started trusting his words, my future began to look great. I stopped doubting and now have been in business since 2011. I stopped doubting and stopped listening to other people's opinions about my life. I allowed God to choose my husband and he gave me the one he wanted for me. If I kept doubting and second guessing myself I would never have gotten anywhere. I had to really trust and believe God and not second guess what he tells me to do. When I stopped asking others for their opinion and followed God's directions everything fell in place. I can't doubt what God tells me. Isaiah 31:1 KJV says woe to them that go down to Egypt for help; and stay on horses, and trust in chariots, because they are many; and in horsemen, because they are very strong; but they look not unto holy one of Israel, neither seek the Lord! In other words, it will be painful if you choose to trust man and doubt God.

# I DECREE AND DECLARE

## (I WILL NOT DOUBT GOD)

## Notes

<h1 style="text-align:center">PART 2</h1>

Wow!!! That's all I can say after reflecting about my old tree. It was a lot more, but I wanted you to get just enough to see that you are not alone. Someone went through what you went through or you are still in. Believe that when you come from just surviving and start dreaming you can BUILD YOUR OWN TREE. I can honestly say today that I have my very own tree, and it starts with me. I just had a moment after typing this. It feels so good to actually type it and believe it. I'm not saying to you it's going to be easy. Roman's 8:28 KJV says And we know that all things work together for good to them that love God, to them who are the called according to his purpose. In other words if you put it in God's hands he will help you BUILD YOUR OWN TREE. By adding these words to my new tree it caused me to be who I am today. Hello I'm a woman that is whole. I am not yet complete because my tree is still growing, but I am an ambassador for Christ, a married woman for 21 years and counting to my knight in shining armor. A mother of 3 beautiful children, an entrepreneur, owner of Ve'Nices Full Figure Boutique NOMINATED AND AWARDED BEST IN RETAIL IN 2018 from NJ BLACK BUSINESSES, Pastor, Mentor, Motivator, speaker and now an author. This is because I learned how to dream. I pray that this will help you get started. I encourage you to BUILD IT. Start Decreeing and Declaring over your new tree. I chose to use bricks for my new tree, because the devil is always trying to blow my branches down. With the bricks I'm laying down a foundation. If you want to know how my tree looks now keep reading.

GALATIONS 5:22 – 23 KJV BUT THE FRUIT OF THE SPIRIT IS:

## LOVE

## 1 Corinthians 13:4-5 NLT

LOVE ENDURES WITH PATIENCE AND SERENITY, LOVE IS KIND AND THOUGHTFUL, AND NOT JEALOUS OR ENVIOUS; LOVE DOES NOT BRAG AND IS NOT PROUD OR ARROGANT. IT IS NOT RUDE; IT IS NOT SELF SEEKING, IT IS NOT PROVOKED [ NOR OVERLY SENSITIVE AND EASILY ANGERED] ; IT DOES NOT TAKE INTO ACCOUNT A WRONG ENDURED.

These are a few definitions of different types of Love in the bible.

Eros (Pronounced Air-ohs) is the Greek word for sensual or romantic love between married couples. Genesis 2:24 KJV

Store (Pronounced Stor-Jay ) is a term of love in the bible between parents and children, and brothers and sisters. Romans 12:10 KJV

Agape (Pronounced UH-GAH-PAY) is the highest type of love in the bible. It's the divine love that comes from God. Agape love is perfect, unconditional, and pure. John 3:16 KJV

Nothing can top the love of God. God has shown me the real meaning of true Love. I didn't think I could feel that kind of love. The closer my relationship with God has become, the more I've learned to love. I learned how to even love my enemies. I had to realize that they don't know that they are being used by the devil. So I pray that they can feel the kind of love that God gives.

## Notes

____________________

____________________

____________________

____________________

____________________

____________________

____________________

____________________

____________________

____________________

____________________

____________________

____________________

____________________

____________________

____________________

____________________

____________________

____________________

# GALATIANS 5: 22- 23 KJV BUT THE FRUIT OF THE  SPIRIT IS…..

## JOY

### James 1:2-3 NLT

DEAR BROTHERS AND SISTERS, WHEN TROUBLES OF ALL KIND COMES YOUR WAYS, CONSIDER IT AN OPPORTUNITY FOR GREAT JOY. FOR YOU KNOW THAT WHEN YOUR FAITH IS TESTED, YOUR ENDURANCE HAS A CHANCE TO GROW.

Joy is a feeling of great pleasure and happiness. I had to understand that the joy is within your heart. The bible says in Nehemiah 8:10, The joy of the Lord is our strength. Do you get it? Joy is equal to strength. This is a must have in your life, to make it through your tests and trials. I use to think that I had to have something good happen to have joy, but that's not true. No matter what happens in your life joy should always be present in your life. In your good times and in your bad times. I know you might wonder how you can have joy in my bad times.  We may not be able to control our circumstances, but we can control how we think about our circumstances. When bad things happen, we can immediately reverse our negative words to positive. For example when trials come, and we say this is terrible or I'm having a bad day, we can change it to I'm having a bad day, but I'm going to get through it.  When you do that you're joy kicks in to give you strength.

**Notes**

## GALATIANS 5:22-23 BUT THE FRUIT OF THE SPIRIT IS.

## PEACE

### 1 Peter 3:11 NLT

## TURN AWAY FROM EVIL AND DO GOOD. SEARCH FOR PEACE, AND WORK TO MAINTAIN IT.

Peace means freedom from disturbance, tranquility. This is something everyone wants, but it's hard to get, because of everyday life. For example bills, family, relationships, careers, etc. Most of all our minds. Peace of mind is important because it can cause you to make some wrong decisions. These decisions will cause pain to everyone around you including yourself. I pray a prayer every day for peace. By doing that I put a command on my day. On how I want my day to be. I have to be honest with you. I'm not saying it always works. We are in a world full of distractions. It's set up to take our peace. We have to stay focused on God to get through life. God is the only way.

# Notes

**4<sup>th</sup>**

GALATIONS 5:22 – 23 KJV BUT THE FRUIT OF THE SPIRIT IS:

**LONGSUFFERING**

**James 4:7 NLT**

SO HUMBLE YOURSELF BEFORE GOD. RESIST THE DEVIL, AND HE WILL FLEE FROM YOU.

Longsuffering is having or showing patience in spite of troubles. When going through my depression it was longsuffering, but with God I was able to get through it. If I didn't have him to lean on I would have taken my life. Mathew 24:13 KJV says But he that shall endure unto the end, the same shall be saved.  I never thought I would make it to this point. Now that I got a taste of experiencing it. GUESS WHAT? It feels good!!!! I had to realize I can't tell people about longsuffering. I can only show them. Despite all the challenges that I have faced I continued to give God all the praise. I didn't know if or when I would get from under this cloud of depression, but always trusted that God could heal me and deliver me. Now that the cloud has been lifted I am still praising him in my new season of peace and joy. The suffering of depression has been lifted. Can I just tell you it feels so good to be in this new season. I am so glad I endured and I am stronger and better because of it.

# Notes

GALATIONS 5:22 – 23 KJV BUT THE FRUIT OF THE SPIRIT IS:

## GENTLENESS

## Proverbs 15:1 NIV

A GENTLE ANSWER TURN AWAY WRATH, BUT A HARSH WORD STIRS UP ANGER.

Gentleness is the quality of being kind, tender, or mild-mannered. This is another stop, look and listen. We have to know that when our sisters and brothers need us. We can't respond the same way to everyone. Everyone is different.  Everyone can't receive harsh criticism in the same manner, even it is true. Some may need you to talk to them with a soft and gentle approach. So we have to be careful how we talk to one another. I know to take time to feel out the person and the situation before I reply, because I want them to do the same way with me. We can be a strong person with a soft and understanding heart.  A lot of relationships and friendship have broken up due to our harsh words. Even though we feel like we are helping them. Like my mother always says that one of our late Bishops use to say. If you hurt, you have to know how to heal. So we have to have a gentleness about us at all times.

# Notes

GALATIONS 5:22 – 23 KJV BUT THE FRUIT OF THE SPIRIT IS:

## GOODNESS

## Nahum 1:7 NIV

THE LORD IS GOOD, A REFUGE IN A TIME OF TROUBLE. HE CARES FOR THOUSE WHO TRUST IN HIM.

Goodness is the quality of being morally good or virtuous. When I experienced the goodness of the Lord. It allowed me to see different. It allowed me to feel different. The difference was that I have him to go to when I feel lost, confused, and second guessing who I am. I always went to people for safety. The Lord let me know in my troubles, I can come to him. When I go to him he gives me unconditional love. I always feel safe with the Lord. His goodness covers me, because of that I'm never alone. I want those that are reading this to ask God to share his goodness over you, and for you to show goodness to others. A goodness that allows you to be kind to others the way God is kind to us.

# Notes

GALATIONS 5:22 – 23 KJV BUT THE FRUIT OF THE SPIRIT IS:

## FAITH

## Matthew 21:22 NLT

YOU CAN PRAY FOR ANYTHING, AND IF YOU HAVE FAITH, YOU WILL RECEIVE IT.

Faith is a strong belief in God. I live by faith, because if I didn't I wouldn't have written this book. Writing this book showed me that only faith could have done it. The Holy Spirit had me to do something I never did before.  I never thought I could do it, but because I trust in the Lord, and had faith I was able to do it. I pray every day that he would give me the words to write. He did just that. Now my new prayer is that, when everyone reads this book that your level of faith gets stronger than it is now.

## Notes

____________________________________________

____________________________________________

____________________________________________

____________________________________________

____________________________________________

____________________________________________

____________________________________________

____________________________________________

____________________________________________

# 8th
# MEEKNESS

GALATIONS 5:22 – 23 KJV BUT THE FRUIT OF THE SPIRIT IS:

## Psalm 37:11 NIV

THE MEEK SHALL INHERIT THE LAND AND ENJOY PEACE AND PROSPERITY.

Meekness means to be humble. It wasn't till I learned and became humble that the doors began to open for me. Meekness taught me how to be grateful and blessed in everything I do. I don't ever want to feel like every blessing I receive is because of me. I pray that I don't get so caught up that I lose my focus and my assignment. God gave me this assignment to write this book, to encourage his people to receive him and build a relationship with him. Yes, you read it right God not me. So he gets all the glory not me. He gets all the praise not me. He gets all the honor NOT ME!

## Notes

__________________________________

__________________________________

__________________________________

__________________________________

__________________________________

__________________________________

__________________________________

**9**th

GALATIONS 5:22 – 23 KJV BUT THE FRUIT OF THE SPIRIT IS:

## TEMPERACE

## 2 Timothy 1:5

FOR GOD GAVE US A SPIRIT NOT OF FEAR BUT OF POWER, LOVE AND SELF-CONTROL

Temperance refers to the ability to have self-control. It is really about allowing the Holy Spirit to have control. When we begin to operate in the fruits of the spirit it shows in our behavior and actions. There was a time that I operated in fear, and that I may not have walked in love, but now that has changed. My desire to please God has me in a place where I want to show and experience everything he has for me.  Before I would allow other people to get me angry and take me out of character. It was difficult for me to show love and be humbled when someone did something to me. What use to take me to a place of wanting to fight no longer does. I would get angry and an ugly side of me would show. I didn't like this side of me because I would be out of control. Now I can take a Selah moment, which is a time to pause. This pause allows me to stop, look and listen instead of reacting. I now allow the Holy Spirit to be my guide and it feels so good.

# Notes

## It's Time to Build

I want to leave you with this. 1 Thessalonians 5; 16-18 NIV say to REJOICE ALWAYS, PRAY CONTINUALLY, GIVE THANKS IN ALL CIRCUMSTANCES, FOR THIS IS GOD'S WILL FOR YOU IN CHRIST JESUS. In other words if you do all these things. God will help you BUILD YOUR OWN TREE. You don't have to stay in the old create your new. No longer should you allow the devil to keep you in bondage. We have to start DECREEING AND DECLARING over our lives. We are more than what man says we are. If man says you are good. You say you are great. If man say you are average. You say you are above average. If man says you are poor. You say you are rich. What I'm trying to say to you is to reverse the negative words to positive, and start believing it. Believe that Greater is here for you and it starts NOW!!!! Like I said in the beginning. You can't plant what you been through, but you can build where you are going!!!!


## LET'S START BUILDING!!!!

www.ingramcontent.com/pod-product-compliance
Lightning Source LLC
Chambersburg PA
CBHW071524030726
47593CB00003B/1384